Jacob of Serugh and His Influence on John of Dara as Exemplified by the Use of Two Verse-Homilies

Analecta Gorgiana

1049

Series Editor

George Anton Kiraz

Analecta Gorgiana is a collection of long essays and short monographs which are consistently cited by modern scholars but previously difficult to find because of their original appearance in obscure publications. Carefully selected by a team of scholars based on their relevance to modern scholarship, these essays can now be fully utilized by scholars and proudly owned by libraries.

Jacob of Serugh and His Influence on John of Dara as Exemplified by the Use of Two Verse-Homilies

Aho Shemunkasho

gorgias press
2011

Gorgias Press LLC, 954 River Road, Piscataway, NJ, 08854, USA

www.gorgiaspress.com

Copyright © 2011 by Gorgias Press LLC

Originally published in 2010

All rights reserved under International and Pan-American Copyright Conventions. No part of this publication may be reproduced, stored in a retrieval system or transmitted in any form or by any means, electronic, mechanical, photocopying, recording, scanning or otherwise without the prior written permission of Gorgias Press LLC.

2011 ܟܒ

ISBN 978-1-4632-0097-8   ISSN 1935-6854

Reprinted from the 2010 Piscataway edition.

Printed in the United States of America

JACOB OF SERUGH AND HIS INFLUENCE ON JOHN OF DARA AS EXEMPLIFIED BY THE USE OF TWO VERSE-HOMILIES

AHO SHEMUNKASHO

1. INTRODUCTION

From the late antiquity onwards, referring to the authors who were in the "orthodox" true faith, became a common method of proving the "truth" and right understanding of theological aspects which were being dealt with. Whereas, Syriac authors of early Syriac Christendom based their knowledge mainly on Holy Scripture, as well as on wisdom found in the created world, and on their social and common experiences in life. When they try to prove their theological arguments, they refer primarily to the Bible, but also to nature. Particularly Jacob of Serugh, as well as Ephrem, sees the revelation of God, next to the Incarnation in human body, in Scripture as well as in nature. Both, Holy Scripture and nature posses divine power that can be revealed to everyone everywhere. Jacob of Serugh's homilies contain frequent allusions to, and citations from the Bible, but also provide references to nature. This however, changed with later writers. In addition to Holy Scripture and nature, later writers look at the texts of previous writers and present what they say. So too many of the later writers often refer to Jacob of Serugh who had a great influence on the Syriac writers following him, as well as on the whole of Syriac Christianity in general. A large number of selected couplets from Jacob's verse-homilies have been incorporated into the liturgical prayers and are chanted in Syriac churches up to today. Jacob has also been cited and referred to by John of Dara who died in 860 AD.

After introducing John of Dara and his work briefly this article, as exemplified, demonstrates only the use of two of Jacob's verse-homilies in John of Dara's treatises found in Codex 356 in Mardin. These are the *Memro On whether Adam was created mortal or immortal* and *Memro On Adam's Expulsion from Paradise*. Both of Jacob's *memre* have been edited and translated into French by Khalil Alwan [= **Alwan**][1] in 1989.

Since most of John of Dara's work has neither been edited nor translated yet, the following manuscripts have been used: Codex 356 from Mardin [= **A**] that could be from the 9th–12th Century; Mingana 67 [= **B**] from 1911 and Damascus Patriarchate 4/4 [= **C**] from 1912. The last two manuscripts (B and C) are copied from the first one (A).

2. JOHN OF DARA AND HIS WORK

Not very much is known about John of Dara[2], but he is supposed to be the West Syriac Metropolitan of Dara who appears in the context of Patriarch Dionysius of Tell-Mahre in the *Chronicle* of Michael the Great.[3] Patriarch Dionysius of Tell-Mahre ordained an Iwannis, a monk from the monastery of St. Hannanjo (Deir Za'faran) near Mardin, as a Metropolitan for Dara in 825 AD, who

---

[1] Alwan, Khalil. *Jacques de Saroug: Quatre Homélies Métriques sur la Création*, CSCO, 508, S.Syr. 214, Lovanii, 1989, 18–77; CSCO, 509, S.Syr. 215, Lovanii, 1989, 17–86.

[2] For John of Dara see Baumstark, Anton. *Geschichte der Syrischen Literatur*, 275–7, Bonn, 1922; Barsoum, Ignatius Aphram I. *The Scattered Pearls. A History of Syriac Literature and sciences*, transl. and ed. by Matti Moosa, 390–2, Piscataway, 2003.

[3] The chronicle of Michael the Great survived in a unique manuscript from Edessa, dated 1599, that is now in Aleppo. A facsimile of it was produced by Gorgias Press in 2008. In 1899 a transcribed copy was prepared for Jean-Baptiste Chabot who published it with a French translation, annotations and indices in Paris 1905–1910: Chabot, J.-B. *Chronique de Michel le Syrien, Patriarche Jacobite d'Antioche (1166–1199)*, I–IV, Paris, 1905–10.

was followed by Athanasius Hakim in 860 AD.[4] In his French translation of Michael the Great's Chronicle Jean-Baptiste Chabot identifies this Iwannis with John of Dara, as he adds in the foot note: "Jean de Dara".[5]

John of Dara is considered to be a "proficient scholar and illustrious theologian"[6] and because of the importance of his treatises, he is often listed among the well known biblical and liturgical West Syriac commentators of late antiquity and early Middle Age.

John of Dara's treatises survived in various Manuscripts, but two of them contain most of his work. These are a manuscript in Mosul and one in Mardin. Other works have also been attributed to him, which may or may not be authentic. These are a treatise *On the Soul*,[7] a Book *On Demons*,[8] a *Commentary on the Gospels*,[9] and an *Anaphora*.[10]

---

[4] Michael the Great's *Chronicle*, Manuscript Aleppo, fol. 382v [Chabot, *Chronique de Michel le Syrien*, IV, 756, fol. 378v], see number 64 in the list: "Patriarch John ordained Metropolitan Athanasius Hakim for Dara" (ܐܬܢܐܣܝܘܣ ܚܟܝܡ ܡܝܛܪܘܦܘܠܝܛܐ ܕܕܪܐ).

[5] Chabot, *Chronique de Michel le Syrien*, III, 43. For Patriarch Dionysius of Tell-Mahre see Abramowski, Rudolf. *Dionysius von Tellmahre. Jakobitischer Patriarch von 818–845. Zur Geschichte der Kirche unter dem Islam*, Abh. für die Kunde des Morgenlandes, XXV/2, Leipzig, 1940; Witakowski, Witold. *The Syriac Chronicle of Pseudo Dionysius of Tel-Mahre. A Study in the History of Historiography*, Diss., Acta Universitatis Upsaliensis, Sudia Semitica Upsaliensia, 9, Uppsala, 1987; Palmer, Andrew. *The Seventh Century in the West-Syrian Chronicles*, Translated Texts for Historians, 15, Liverpool, 1993.

[6] Barsoum, *The Scattered Pearls*, 390. See also Edsman, Carl-Martin. "Death, Corruption and Eternal Life," *Bulletin of the Iranian Culture Foundation*, 1 (1969): 85–104 [*On John of Dara, On Resurrection*, p. 89].

[7] The treatise *On the Soul* has been considered to belong rather to Moses bar Kepha. In 1928 Giuseppe Furlani published an article about John of Dara's treatise *On the Soul* based on the text found in Vat. Library, Vat Syr. 147, fol. 133r–168v, from 1234. He also translated it into Italian. Vat Syr. 147, fol. 3r up to 91r, contains Moses bar Kepha's treatise *On the Soul*. The oldest copy could be Vatican MS 100 from the 9th century. The Houghton Library at Harvard University contains an old copy of this

In the manuscript found in the library of the Syrian orthodox bishopric in Mosul, belonging to the 12th or 13th century, consisting of 323 pages,[11] we find altogether eleven treatises (*memre*)[12] and a

---

treatise, MS 3973 (104 pages). In 1999, J. Reller wrote an article showing the relation of John of Dara's texts and understanding of the soul towards Moses bar Kepha and Bar Hebraeus, see Reller, Jobst. "Iwannis von Dara, Mose bar Kepha und Barhebräus über die Seele, traditionsgeschichtlich untersucht," in Reinink, G.J., and A.C. Klugkist, ed. *After Bardaisan, Studies on Continuity and Change in Syriac Christianity in Honour of Professor Han J.W. Drijvers*, 253–64, Leuven, 1999. However, it has been assumed that this text doesn't belong to John of Dara, but to Moses bar Kepha.

[8] We find the book *On Demons* under the name of John of Dara in a codex which stems from the 16th or 17th century. The MS in Mardin 381 contains a corpus of theological works of Moses bar Kepha and includes the book *On Demons* in 23 *kephalaia*.

[9] Bar Salibi speaks in his introduction to his *Gospel's Commentary* of the previous commentaries he used for his composition. He mentions John of Dara explicitly when he says: ܗܘܐ ܕܝܢ ܡܢ ܩܕܡܝܐ ܢܝܫܐ ܘܦܘܫܩܐ ܕܣܒܘܬܐ. ܕܡܪܝ ܐܦܪܝܡ ܘܡܪܝ ܝܥܩܘܒ ܕܗܘ̇ ܗ̇ܘ ܕܒܡܠܦܢܘܬܐ ܡܣܬܝܟ. ܘܡܢܐ ܘܡܝܩܪܐ ܘܡܪܝ ܦܝܠܘܟܣܝܢܘܣ ܘܕܩܕܝܫܐ ܐܦܝܣܩܘܦܐ ܕܕܪܐ. See Sedlacek, I., et I.-B. Chabot. *Dionysii bar Salibi Commentarii in Evangelia*, 1, CSCO, 77; S.Syr., 33, Louvain, 1953.

[10] According to I.A. Barsoum an *Anaphora* is also attributed to John of Dara, *The Scattered Pearls*, 392.

[11] A copy of it can be found in the Mingana collection in Birmingham, MS 56. Mingana 56 is a copy of MS Mosul, but without pages 288–323 that are partly difficult to read and do not seem that all of them belong to John of Dara. They look like a collection of biblical verses and passages from various Church Fathers, such as from Severius (p. 321–3). Vat MS 100, transcribed before the year 932, is the oldest codex, but it does not contain all the twelve *kephalaia* found in Mosul codex. Vat MS 100 begins with the four *memre* on resurrection, followed by the *memre* on the celestial hierarchies and the priesthood.

[12] Treatise 1 and 2 are commentaries on celestial and ecclesiastical hierarchy and 3 to 6 on priesthood in reference to Dionysius Areopagite. All 6 *memre* also survived in a manuscript from 1654 AD that is in Oxford Bodleian, Orient. 264, resp. Syr. 152; see Payne-Smith, R. *Catalogues Codd. Syr. Bodleian*, coll. 486–96, Oxonii, 1864.

collection of various texts at the end: two *memre* are on celestial and ecclesiastical hierarchy[13], four on priesthood and priests[14], another four on resurrection of human bodies[15], and one on the offering of the holy mysteries[16]. The title of the final one is not identified.

---

[13] Barsoum, *The Scatered Pearls*, 392: "An eloquent treatise on the policy of the church and the settlement of peace in it, consisting of 39 pages. There is an anonymous copy of this treatise fixed at the end of his book on the theology in the former Mosul manuscript. This treatise is undoubtedly the work of this erudite metropolitan which he wrote in the days of the Patriarch John IV (around 850). We also have an accord copy of the treatise in nineteen pages, transcribed in 1603, which is most probably a reply to Basils II, Maphryono of the East (848–858)." See Strothmann, Werner. *Das Sakrament der Myronweihe in der Schrift de Ecclesiastica Hiearchia des Pseudo Areopagita in syrischen Übersetzungen und Kommentaren*, 49–57, Wiesbaden, 1978.

[14] In some manuscripts the *memre* on the priesthood and priests have been attributed to John Maron. See Varghese, Baby. *John of Dara Commentary on the Eucharist*, Moran Etho, 12, Kerala, 1999; Sader, Jean. "Jean de Dara," in *Dictionnaire de Spiritualité*, VIII, 467–68, Paris, 1974; Breydy, Michel. *La doctrine Syro-Antiochene sur le sacerdoce dans sa version maronite*, Jounieh, 1977; P. Zingerle gives a summary of this work, Zingerle, P. "Aus dem Handschriftlichen syrischen Werk des Johannes von Dara über das Priestertum," *Theologische Quartalschrift* 49 (1867): 183–205; 50 (1868): 267–85.

[15] Moses Bar Kepha has got exactly the same number of *kephaleia* on resurrection as John of Daras' *memro* one, two and three on resurrection, namely all together 34 *kaphalaia* of resurrection. See Strothmann, W. *Moses Bar Kepha, Myron-Weihe*, I, 25, Reihe Syiaca, 7, Wiesbaden 1973. The first three *memre* on resurrection can be found in the following MSs: Vat Syr 100 and 582, Charfet 28, Mingana 56. In his article on "Death, Corruption and Eternal Life" C.-M. Edsman refers to *memro* two on resurrection that discusses the difference between the earthly body and the heavenly one. Quotations are found in Braun, O. "Beiträge zur Geschichte der Eschatologie in den syrischen Kirchen," *Zeitschrift für katholische Theologie*, 16 (1892): 273–91.

[16] This *memro* is a commentary on the liturgy which has been edited by Sader, J. *Le De Oblatione de Jean de Dara*, CSCO, 308; S.Syr., 132, Louvain, 1970, and translated into French, *Le De Oblatione de Jean de*

However, these treatises have not been considered for this article. The result of this work is based on the manuscript found in Mardin, MS 356. It is divided into seven *memre* that are written in fine *Estrangelo* script in 254 pages. The colophon is lost, missing the first three and half *kephalaia* of *memro* one. This parchment codex could be from 9th—12th Century.[17] This codex has been copied at least twice:[18] one copy is in Damascus, copied in *Dayro d-Nutpho* near Mardin, by Dayroyo Michael bar Jeshu' in 1911, except *memro* 6, which has been copied by Dayroyo Johannon; the other copy is in Birmingham (Mingana MS 67), produced by Deacon Mattai bar Paulus in Mosul in 1912.[19]

Dara, CSCO, 309; S.Syr., 133, Louvain, 1970. In 1999, Baby Varghese translated it into English. See Varghese, Baby. *West Syrian Liturgical Theology*, 29–34.

[17] See Vööbus, Anthon. "Important manuscript discoveries of Iwannis of Dara and his literary heritage," *Journal of the American Oriental Society* 96 (1976): 576–8. On page 577 he writes: "This is a codex which has found its hiding place in the monastery of Mar Hannanya ...—unique and priceless records which have not survived elsewhere. The manuscript in question is MS Mardin Orth. 356, written on parchment. Because it has lost its colophon it does not instruct us more precisely about its age, but on palaeographical grounds it can be assigned to the 9th or 10th century. It is astounding to discover that all the works preserved in this collection are new."

[18] According to Vööbus also MS Vat. Syr. 581 is a copy from the same MS. See Vööbus, "Important manuscript," 577.

[19] In 1912 the Damascus manuscript was copied in *Dayro d-Nutpho* that is the monastery of *Yoldath Aloho* near *Dayro d-Mor Hannanyo*, Deir Za'faran in Mardin (see the note on page C 241: ܒܚܕ ܓܠܝ ܒܝܕ ܕܝܪܝܐ ܡܝܟܐܝܠ ܒܪ ܝܫܘܥ ܩܠܝܠܐ ܥܡ ܕܝܪܐ ܕܢܛܦܐ ܩܘܪܝܬܐ). A year before, in 1911, the codex of Mardin was taken to Mosul by the Priest Aphram Barsoum (later Patriarch) and was copied by Deacon Mattai Bar Paulus. This copy is Mingana MS 67. (Also Mingana 56 was copied by the same deacon in 1912). He informs us about the condition of the codex that not all the text was legible and therefore he left gaps for the passages that he couldn't read or were not available. And because Deacon Mattai Bar Paulus had to write it quickly (as he says "by night") it could contain some mistakes according to him: ܐܘ ܐܝܬ ܩܠܝܐ

The manuscript is divided into seven *memre*, which make up a unit: five *kephalaia* on Paradise, nineteen on creation, eight against heretics, thirty-three on resurrection (Easter), eleven on Pentecost[20], eleven on finding of the cross, and nineteen on the divine economy.

3. JOHN OF DARA'S REFERENCES TO JACOB OF SERUGH

In the seven treatises found in the manuscript in Mardin, John of Dara mentions a great number of authors, and occasionally their works. John refers explicitly to nine of them more frequently. These are: John the Solitary (4 times), Basil of Alexandrian (6), Cyril of Alexandrian (6), John Crysostomos (7), Ephrem the Syrian (10), Severios of Antioch (14), Gregory of Nyssa (16), Philoxenos of Mabbug (17) and Jacob of Serugh (19). Indeed, John of Dara uses citations from Jacob of Serugh more than the others.

So far seven verse-homilies of Jacob of Serugh have been identified in John's work, manuscript Mardin 356. These are the *memre*: *On whether Adam was created mortal or immortal*,[21] *On Adam's Expulsion from Paradise*,[22] *On Crucifixion*,[23] *On Resurrect-*

[Syriac text]

(B 178v). For both writers it was indeed a great challenge to copy Mardin MS 356. For a critical edition, their interpretation could help us to read the passages better that have been further damaged since then.

[20] See Vööbus, A. "Die Entdeckung von Überresten der altsyrischen Apostelgeschichte," *Oriens Christianus* 64 (1980): 32–5.

[21] A 46v, B 62r–62v, C 173–75.

[22] A 13r, 21v, 34r, 35v; B 12r, 24v–25r, 43r, 45v; C 38, 72, 121, 129.

[23] Jacob of Serugh's verse-homily *On Crucifixion* ([Syriac]) is structured according to the liturgy of the holy week and it is very long. It is edited under number 53 in Bedjan, Paul. *Homiliae selecae Mar Jacobi Sarugensis*, 2, 447–610. Paris, 1906. The citations found by John of Dara are equivalent to Bedjan's text, pages 588 onwards that is the text *For the Vigil of Holy Saturday* ([Syriac]) and *For the Vigil of the Easter*

ion,[24] *On Ascension*,[25] *On Pentecost and the Distribution of Tongues*[26] and *On Adai and Abgar*.[27]

Referring to Jacob of Serugh, John of Dara does not use the name *Serugh* at all, instead he speaks of Jacob of Batnan (ܝܥܩܘܒ ܕܒܛܢܢ), or sometimes just of Jacob (ܝܥܩܘܒ). In addition John uses respectfully some titles for Jacob, as he calls him Mor (ܡܪܝ), blessed one (ܛܘܒܢܐ), teacher (ܡܠܦܢܐ) and saint (ܩܕܝܫܐ). The following table contains the way John of Dara refers to Jacob of Serugh:

Manuscripts			John of Dara's references to Jacob of Serugh
A	B	C	
13r	12r	38	ܘ[ܐܦ] ܝܥܩܘܒ ܕܒܛܢܢ ܐܡܪ ܒܡܐܡܪܐ ܕ [ܡܛܠ] ܡܦܩܬܗ ܕܐܕܡ ܡܢ ܦܪܕܝܣܐ ܐܡܪ Also Jacob of Batnan said in the *memro* On Adam's Expulsion from Paradise ...

Sunday (ܕܚܕ ܒܫܒܐ ܕܩܝܡܬܐ). The references to Jacob of Serugh's verse-homilies are given in square brackets, whereas the other references refer to John of Dara's manuscripts: **A** 28r–28v, 35v, 64r–64v, 65r–65v, 66v–67r, 78r; **B** 35r, 45v, 86r, 87v, 90r, 105r; **C** 100, 129, 241, 243, 250, 292 [Bedjan II, 588, 592, 595, 600, 603–4].

[24] A 63, 68v, 71r, 80v; B 86r, 92r–92v, 95v, 109v; C 239, 256, 265, 304 [Bedjan II, 600 ff.]

[25] A 35v–36r; B 46r; C 129.

[26] A 93v; B 129r; C 357 [Bedjan II, 677].

[27] A 93v; B 129v; C 357. Jacob's memro *On Addai the Apostle and Abgar the King of Edessa* (ܥܠ ܐܕܝ ܫܠܝܚܐ ܘܐܒܓܪ ܡܠܟܐ) came to us in Vatican's manuscript 117 under *memro* Nr. 108, fol. 268r–270v. It seems that the end of it is missing. The text of folio 271r–271v gives the end of the *memro* On the Camel and needle's eye (ܡܟܐ ܕܢܐܠ ܠܗ ܠܓܡܠܐ ܕܢܥܘܠ ܒܚܪܘܪܐ ܕܡܚܛܐ ܐܘ ܠܥܬܝܪܐ ܠܡܠܟܘܬܐ ܕܐܠܗܐ). There is a translation of a part of it by Messo, Johny. "The Toponym 'Aramea' [ܐܪܡ] in Two Early Syriac Writers (Part I)," *Mardutho d-Suryoye* 19:59 (Oct.-Dec. 2007): 25–7. John of Dara quotes only a few couplets from this *memro*:

Manuscripts			John of Dara's references to Jacob of Serugh
A	B	C	
21v	24v	72–73	ܝܥܩܘܒ ܕܝܢ ܕܒܛܢܢ ܒܡܐܡܪܐ ܕܥܠ ܡܦܩܬܗ ܕܐܕܡ ܡܢ ܦܪܕܝܣܐ ܐܡܪ. ܕܣܛܢܐ ܡܠܠ ܒܚܘܝܐ. ܗܝ ܕܠܗ ܫܠܡܝܢ ܘܣܚ. ܐܡܪ ܓܝܪ ... ܘܐܡܪ ܠܘܩܒܠܗܘܢ. Jacob of Batnan, however, said in the *memro* On Adam's Expulsion from Paradise that Satan spoke through the Serpent. We agree with this. He said… And he said against them indeed ...
28r	35r	100	ܘܗܕܐ ܡܠܦ ܝܥܩܘܒ ܕܒܛܢܢ ܒܡܐܡܪܐ ܗܘ ܕܙܩܝܦܘܬܐ. ܐܡܪ ܓܝܪ ܗܟܢܐ This teaches Jacob of Batnan in the *memro* On Crucifixion. He said so indeed …
34r	43r	121	ܘܝܥܩܘܒ ܕܒܛܢܢ ܐܡܪ And Jacob of Batnan says …
35v	45v	129	ܘܣܗܕ[ܐ] ܠܗܕܐ ܝܥܩܘܒ ܒܡܐܡܪܐ ܕܙܩܝܦܘܬܐ ܟܕ ܐܡܪ And Jacob witnesses this in the *memro* On Crucifixion as he says …
35v	46r	129	ܘܐܢ ܠܐ ܗܟܢܐ ܗܝ: ܣܪܝܩ ܗܘ ܗܘ ܡܐܡܪܐ ܕܥܠ ܟܪܘܒܐ ܘܓܝܣܐ: ܘܐܝܠܝܢ ܕܐܡܪ ܬܘܒ ܝܥܩܘܒ ܒܡܐܡܪܐ ܕܙܩܝܦܘܬܐ. ܘܡܚܘܐ ܕܚܕ ܡܢ ܟܪܘܒܐ ܗܘܐ ܗܘ ܕܡܠܠ ܥܡ ܓܝܣܐ. ܡܢ ܚܝܠܘܬܐ ܕܡܠܐܟܐ ܐܡܪ ܟܬܒܐ ܫܪܝܪܐܝܬ ܘܝܥܩܘܒ ܒܡܐܡܪܐ ܕܣܘܠܩܐ ܐܡܪ And if it is not like this, then the *memro* On the Cherub and Robber and what Jacob said again in the *memro* On Crucifixion is in vain. [Jacob] demonstrates that it was one of the cherubs who talked to the robber. It was one of the angelic hosts, said the [Holy] Scripture said truly. And Jacob says in the *memro* On Accession …

Manuscripts			John of Dara's references to Jacob of Serugh
A	B	C	
46v	62r	173	ܝܥܩܘܒ ܕܝܢ ܒܡܐܡܪܐ ܗܘ ܕܥܠ ܗܿܝ ܕܐܢ ܡܝܘܬܐ ܐܬܒܪܝ ܐܕܡ ܐܘ ܠܐܡܝܘܬܐ Jacob, however, [says] in the *memro* On whether Adam was created mortal or immortal …
46v–47r	62v	175	ܐܝܟܢܐ ܕܡ̈ܠܦܢܐ ܗܠܝܢ ܕܡܣܗܕܝܢ ܡܢ ܠܥܠ ܩܕܡܝܢ As the teachers witness these said above …
63v	86r	239	ܢܛܘܪ̈ܐ ܕܝܢ ܐܡܪ ܝܥܩܘܒ ܕܒܛܢܢ܆ ܕܐܬܚܙܝ ܠܗܘܢ ܢܘܗܪܐ ܕܕܢܚ. Jacob of Badnan, however, said that the shining light was seen by the [grave/tomb's] keepers …
64r	87r	241	ܝܥܩܘܒ ܕܝܢ ܒܡܐܡܪܐ ܕܙܩܝܦܘܬܐ ܐܡܪ. .... Jacob, however, says in the *memro* On Crucifixion …
64v	87r	242	ܘܐܡܪܝܢܢ ... ܐܝܟ ܕܐܡܪ ܡܪܝ ܝܥܩܘܒ And we say, … as Mor Jacob said …
65r	87v	243	ܕܝܥܩܘܒ ܒܡܐ̄ ܪܒܐ ܕܙܩܝܦܘܬܐ: Jacob in the great *memro* On Crucifixion ….
66v	90r	250	ܕܝܥܩܘܒ ܒܡܐ̄ ܕܙܩܝܦܘܬܐ ܕܒܦܘܠܓܐ ܗܘ ܕܩܕܡܝܬܐ: Jacob in the *memro* On Crucifixion, first part …
68v	92r	256	ܐܡܪ ܓܝܪ ܡܕܝܢܐ ܝܥܩܘܒ Jacob says indeed ...
71r	95v	265	ܒܪܡ ܝܥܩܘܒ ܕܒܛܢܢ ܐܡܪ But Jacob of Batnan says …
78r	105r	292	ܘܝܥܩܘܒ ܬܘܒ ܒܡܐܡܪܐ ܕܙܩܝܦܘܬܐ ܡܚܘܐ And Jacob demonstrates again in the *memro* On Crucifixion …

Manuscripts			John of Dara's references to Jacob of Serugh
A	B	C	
81r	109v	303	ܐܝܟ ܕܓܪܝܓܘܪܝܘܣ ܕܢܘܣܐ. ܘܡܪܝ ܝܥܩܘܒ ܘܐܦܪܝܡ As Gregorios of Nyssa and Mor Jacob and Ephrem ...
93v	129r–129v	357	ܠܗܠܝܢ ܣܗܕ ܛܘܒܢܐ ܝܥܩܘܒ ܒܡܐܡܪܐ ܕܦܘܠܓ ܠܫܢܐ ܟܕ ܐܡܪ ... ܘܬܘܒ And the blessed Jacob witnesses these while he says in the *memro* On Distribution of Tongues ... And again [he says] ...
93v	129v	357	ܗܕܐ ܡܚܘܐ ܡܪܝ ܝܥܩܘܒ ܒܡܐܡܪܐ ܕܥܠ ܐܒܓܪ ܘܐܕܝ. ܐܡܪ ܓܝܪ Mor Jacob demonstrates this in the *memro* On Abgar and Addai. He said indeed ...

It is worth mentioning that before quoting from Jacob, John often uses the verb "to say", which appears in both forms, as a perfect (ܐܡܪ) and participle (ܐܡܪ). Occasionally, Jacob does not use a verb at all, he just mentions the author Jacob before he cites the text. It becomes obvious from the context that John not just agree with Jacob, but rather he presents him as an authority who confirms his own theological thought. However, when he wants to highlight Jacob's teaching, he uses the verbs "to demonstrate" (ܡܚܘܐ), "to witness" (ܣܗܕ) and "to teach" (ܡܠܦ). All three verbs appear as participles implying the continuous importance of Jacob's teaching.

Further, John distinguishes Jacob's authority with the particles ܕܝܢ, ܓܝܪ, ܐܦ. When he quotes from Jacob in order to approve what he, have said or other authors he uses the particle ܐܦ. In turn, when he wants to contradict other authors, John introduces Jacob with the particle ܕܝܢ, sometimes ܓܝܪ follows as an indication that what Jacob teaches is at the same time of more value than some of the other authors. Generally, with the particle ܓܝܪ John emphasises Jacob's authority and the importance of understanding the topics dealt with correctly.

3.1. Homily on whether Adam was created mortal or immortal

The text of Jacob's verse-homily *On whether Adam was created mortal or immortal* given below is based on manuscript Mardin 137, number 281, folio 239v–243r, and it is compared to Alwan's edition. Using manuscript Mardin 137 [= **E**] and Sharfeh 312, Alwan edited this verse-homily in 1989. In addition he used also two other fragments[28] and an Arabic translation of it.[29] Vööbus already identified this verse-homily in these manuscripts and part of it in some fragments.[30]

Jacob of Serugh's verse-homily contains 308 lines. John of Dara quotes 33 lines[31] of them in *memro* three, chapter three that is entitled "[Objection] of [the followers of] Julian [of Halicarnassus] and their excess/intemperance" (ܒܪܬ ܝܘܠܝܢܐ ܘܡܫܘܚܪܗܘܢ).[32] Julian of Halicarnassus, a contemporary of Severios of Antioch, taught that Christ's body became incorruptible and immortal due to the union with the Word of God.[33] *Memro* three includes further heresies, like Simeonism, Manicheism, Nestorianism, and some theories on the Tree of Life. John of Dara rejects all theories that blame the Creator for the fall of man and which see evil in the nature of

---

[28] Alwan, 18–30; French translation, 17–32. In his introduction Alwan describes the manuscripts he used, see pages xviii–xlvii. As fragments Alwan used also MS British Library, Add 14532 and Add. 12155.

[29] For the description of the Arabic translation Alwan, CSCO, 508; S.Syr., 214. Lovanii, 1989, ix–xviii.

[30] A. Vööbus already identified this verse-homily in these manuscripts. See Vööbus, A. *Handschriftliche Überlieferung der Memre-Dichtung des Ja`qob von Serug*, II, 23. CSCO, 345; Subsidia, 40, Louvain, 1973; IV, 31, CSCO, 422; Subsidia, 61, Louvain, 1980.

[31] Jacob of Serugh's verse-homily *On whether Adam was created mortal or immortal* (ܐܦܢ ܗܘܐ ܐܕܡ ܡܢ ܟܕ ܐܬܒܪܝ ܡܝܘܬܐ ܐܘ ܠܐ ܡܝܘܬܐ) is found under *Memro* 281 in MS Mardin 137, folio 239v–243r. John of Dara refers to this *Memro* in A 46v, B 62r–62v, C 173–75 [E 239v–243r].

[32] Chapter three: ܩܦܠܐܘܢ ܕܬܠܬܐ: ܘܫܘܚܪܗܘܢ ܕܝܘܠܝܢܝܣܛܐ.

[33] See Grillmeier, Alois, and Theresia Hainthaler. *Christ in Christian Tradition: From the Council of Chalcedon (451) to Gregory the Great (590–604)*, II, 25–6. 1995.

created beings, such as in the Tree of Life, in the Serpent or even in God's commandment. According to John, Julian's theory on the nature of the created human beings is that Adam's body was created immortal as his soul. Thus, according to Julian the immortality of man was not a divine gift by mercy, but it was naturally real, and man would have remained "uncorrupted" (ܠܐ ܡܬܚܒܠܢܐ), passionless/without suffering (ܠܐ ܚܫܘܫܐ) and immortal (ܠܐ ܡܝܘܬܐ), if he had not trespassed against the divine commandment (ܥܒܪ ܦܘܩܕܢܐ).[34] Death of the soul (ܡܝܘܬܐ ܕܢܦܫܐ) is understood as separation of man from his Creator by sin, and bodily death (ܡܝܘܬܐ ܕܦܓܪܐ) is the separation of man from natural life (ܦܘܪܫܢܐ ܕܡܢ ܚܝ̈ܐ ܡܬܝܪ̈ܐ ܠܟܝܢܐ).

Rejecting Julian's theory, John of Dara emphasises the mortality of the human physical nature according to its creation, and its immortality as a divine gift according to divine grace. If Adam was physically immortal he would have remained immortal even after he sinned, like Satan. The soul was immortal and remained immortal even after death, but the body was mortal and was kept immortal by grace only until Adam became disobedient. In this context, John refers briefly to Cyril of Alexandria, Dionysius Areopagita and Athanasius, but the long reference to Jacob's *memro* *"On whether Adam was created mortal or immortal"* is noticeable. John writes: [35]

ܡܛܘܠ ܕܝܢ ܕܡܐܡܪܐ ܗܘ ܕܥܠ ܗܝ ܕܐܢ ܡܝܘܬܐ ܐܬܒܪܝ ܐܕܡ ܐܘ ܠܐ ܡܝܘܬܐ:

39– ܐܢ ܡܝܘܬܐ[36] ܣܝܡ ܗܘܐ ܕܠܡܘܬܐ ܩܡ ܥܒܕܗ.
40 ܠܡܢܐ ܝܗܒ ܥܠܬܐ ܕܡܝܘܬܐ[37] ܒܗܘ ܐܝܠܢܐ.

[34] See *Memro* three, the beginning of chapter three.

[35] The numbers of the right side refer to the lines of Jacob's *memro* which are identical with Alwan's edition. The footnotes contain the variations and differences found between John of Dara's text (A, B, C), Jacob of Serugh text (E) and Alwan's edition. A 46v, B 62r, C 173. See Alwan, *memro* two, 18ff.

[36] ܐܢ ܡܝܘܬܐ: BC missing.

[37] ܕܡܝܘܬܐ: Alwan ܕܡܝܘܬܗ.

41– ܘܐܦ ܒܟܝܢܗ ܠܐ ܡܫܘܬܐ ܒܪܢܫܗ، ܡܕܪܟܬ.[38]
42 ܐܝܟܢܐ ܡܒܝܬ[39] ܘܪܟܝܫ، ܒܫܘܬܐ ܠܠܐ ܡܫܘܬܐ.
43– ܐܦ ܡܟܐܬ ܗܘܐ ܕܗ ܠܐ ܢܐܟܘܠ ܡܢ ܐܝܠܢܐ.
44 ܢܛܪܬܐ[40] ܗܘܬ ܗ̇ܝ، ܕܐܬܦܩܕ ܡܢ ܒܪܘܝܗ.
45– ܘܐܦ ܒܟܝܢܗ ܚܠܬܐ ܠܒܫܘܬܗ[41] ܠܐ ܐܬܬܒܪܬ.
46 ܠܐ ܡܟܐܬ ܗܘܐ ܘܠܐ ܕܗ ܢܐܟܘܠ ܡܢ ܐܝܠܢܐ.
47– ܕܗܐ ܩܛܠܢܐ ܠܐ ܡܫܘܬܐ ܘܠܐ ܡܢܝܐ ܡܟܐܬ.[42]
48 ܘܡܕ ܦܘܩܕܢܐ ܠܐ ܢܛܪ ܡܬܚܬܘܡ ܗܘ ܕܗ ܒܛܠܝܐ.
49– ܟܕܒܪܐ ܘܪܫܥܐ ܕܬܫܥܬ ܡܘܬܐ ܗܝܡܢܝܢ ܟܠܗܘܢ.
50 ܘܠܗ[43] ܦܘܩܕܢܐ ܟܬܒܘ[44] ܐܝܟ ܐܕܡ ܘܟܠ ܗܕܐ ܡܒܝܬܘ.

55– ܡܕܡ ܕܐܒܘܗܝ، ܠܐ ܡܫܘܬܐ ܡܢ ܥܘܪܢܐ.[45]
56 ܠܐ ܡܢܝܐ ܒܫܘܬܐ ܡܬܦܪܥ ܠܗ ܘܠܐ ܕܗ ܢܛܠܐ.[46]

131– ܒܗ̇ ܒܟܒܝܠܬܗ ܐܝܟ ܬܬܒܝܢ[47] ܢܠܦ ܐܝܬ ܗܘ.
132 ܕܐܦ ܡܫܘܬܐ ܘܠܐ ܡܫܘܬܐ ܐܬܪܒܒ ܗܘܐ.

141– ܐܬܢܨܚܬ ܠܗ ܡܢ ܝܐܪܘܬܗ[48] ܠܡܐܢܐ ܡܠܝܠܐ.
142 ܕܗܘ ܢܟܒܐ ܠܗ ܡܫܘܬܐ ܘܫܢܝܐ ܐܝܟ ܢܟܝܠܗ.

157– ܐܝܬ ܗܘܐ ܒܗ ܚܢ ܚܠܬܐ ܕܒܫܘܬܗ[49] ܕܡܢ ܕܢܝܫܐ ܗܘ.
158 ܘܐܝܬ ܗܘܐ ܠܗ[50] ܬܘܒ ܐܬܪܐ ܕܫܢܝܐ[51] ܕܠܦܝܡ ܪܘܚܐ ܗ̇ܝ.

---

[38] ܡܕܪܟܬ: Alwan, E ܡܕܪܟܐܬ.

[39] B add ܐܕܡ.

[40] ܢܛܪܬܐ: Alwan, E ܢܛܪܐ.

[41] ܠܒܫܘܬܗ: Alwan ܠܒܫܘܬܐ.

[42] ܕܗܐ ܩܛܠܢܐ ܠܐ ܡܫܘܬܐ ܘܠܐ ܡܢܝܐ ܡܟܐܬ: Alwan, E ܗܐ ܩܛܠܢܐ ܕܠܘ ܡܫܘܬܐ ܗܘ ܠܐ ܡܢܝܐ ܡܟܐܬ.

[43] ܘܠܗ: B ܘܠܐ ; Alwan, E ܘܠ.

[44] ܟܬܒܘ: Alwan ܟܬܒܘܗ.

[45] ܠܐ ܡܫܘܬܐ ܡܢ ܥܘܪܢܐ: E ܡܢ ܥܘܪܢܐ ܠܐ ܡܫܘܬܐ. In the main text Alwan has got the same as John of Dara.

[46] ܡܬܦܪܥ ܠܗ ܘܠܐ ܕܗ ܢܛܠܐ: Alwan, E ܡܬܦܪܥ ܠܗ ܘܠܐ ܕܗ ܒܛܝܠܐ.

[47] ܬܬܒܝܢ: Alwan, E ܬܬܒܢܐ.

[48] ܐܬܢܨܚܬ ܠܗ ܡܢ ܝܐܪܘܬܗ: Alwan, E ܐܬܢܨܚܬ ܠܗ ܐܦ ܝܐܪܘܬܐ.

[49] ܚܠܬܐ ܕܒܫܘܬܗ: Alwan, E ܚܠܬܐ ܠܒܫܘܬܐ.

[50] ܘܐܝܬ ܗܘܐ ܠܗ: A ܘܐܝܬ ܗܘܐ ; Alwan, E ܘܐܝܬ ܗܘܐ ܒܗ.

[51] ܕܫܢܝܐ : Alwan, E ܠܫܢܝܐ.

159– ܐܠܘ ܪܒܐ ܗܘܐ ܘܡܟܐ ܕܢܗܘܐ ܠܐ ܡܝܘܬܐ܀
160 ܬܘܦܬܐ ܗܘܬ ܠܗ ܢܥܒܐ ܠܦܓܪܐ ܕܠܐܚܝܐ[52] ܓܒܠܗ.
161 ܘܬܚܒ[53] ܥܡܠܐ ܘܒܪܥܘܬܗ ܥܪܒ[54] ܥܡ ܡܝܘܬܐ.

197– ܘܟܕ ܚܐܪܘܬܐ ܡܠܟܬ ܦܐܪܐ[55] ܡܢ ܐܝܠܢܐ.
198 ܘܚܝܘܗܝ ܗܘܐ ܡܝܘܬܐ ܠܗܘ ܕܐܠܘ ܢܛܪ ܠܐ ܡܟܐܬ ܗܘܐ.

279– ܒܐܝܕܘܗܝ[56] ܣܡܗ ܠܓܠܠܬ ܚܝܐ ܘܐܫܠܡܬ ܡܝܘܬܐ܀[57]
280 ܘܝܗܒ ܠܗ ܐܬܪܐ ܕܐܠܗܘܬܐ ܕܢܗܘܐ ܠܗ ܠܬܘܪܒ.

281– ܐܠܘ ܒܒܪܝܗ ܠܐ ܡܝܘܬܐ ܡܢ ܫܘܪܝܐ.
282 ܡܢܐ ܕܒܥܐ ܗܘܐ ܥܠ ܦܘܩܕܢܐ ܐܡܓܪ[58] ܗܘܐ ܠܗ.

283– ܘܐܠܘ ܒܪܢܫܐ ܗܘܐ ܬܘܒ ܡܝܘܬܐ ܐܝܟ ܚܝܘܬܐ.
284 ܡܢܐ ܢܛܪ ܗܘܐ ܡܢ ܦܘܩܕܢܐ ܕܢܛܪ ܗܘܐ ܠܗ.

285– ܥܒܪ ܡܚܝܠ ܗܘܐ ܡܝܘܬܐ ܘܠܐ ܡܝܘܬܐ.
286 ܘܠܚܐܪܘܬܐ ܝܗܒ ܫܘܠܛܢܐ ܥܠ ܬܪܬܝܗܝܢ܀

"Jacob [says], however, in the *memro* that is *On whether Adam was created mortal or immortal:*[59]

If Adam was supposed to be made mortal by his Maker, 39–
then why did He put the cause of death in that tree? 40

And if he was created immortal by nature first, 41–
then how did he die, and death defeat the immortal one. 42

If he was going to die although he had not eaten from the tree, 43–
then it was too much, that he has been commanded by his Creator. 44

---

52 ܕܠܐܚܝܐ: B ܕܚܝܐ .

53 ܘܬܚܒ: Alwan, E ܘܕܚܒ.

54 ܥܪܒ: Alwan, E ܢܬܒ.

55 ܥܪܒ: Alwan, E ܢܬܒ.

56 ܦܐܪܐ: Alwan, A ܒܐܪܐ.

57 ܠܓܠܠܬ ܚܝܐ ܘܐܫܠܡܬ ܡܝܘܬܐ : E ܠܐܫܠܡܬ ܚܝܐ ܘܓܠܠܬ ܡܝܘܬܐ; Alwan ܠܐܫܠܡܬ ܚܝܐ ܘܓܠܠܬܐ ܕܡܝܘܬܐ.

58 ܐܡܓܪ: A ܠܡܓܪ ; Alwan, E ܡܓܪ.

59 A 46v, B 59–60, C 173: ܝܥܩܘܒ ܕܝܢ ܒܡܐܡܪܐ ܗܘ ܕܥܠ ܗܿܝ ܕܐܢ ܡܝܘܬܐ ܐܬܒܪܝ ܐܕܡ ܐܘ ܠܐ ܡܝܘܬܐ.

And if the cause of death was not created in his nature,	45–
he would not die, even though he ate from the tree,	46
For, behold, Satan is immortal and cannot die.	47–
And although he never keeps the commandment, he is alive and misleads [people].	48
Animals and creatures are an object to death every day,	49–
and they die, even though they never trespass the commandment as Adam did.	50
That what immortal is from beginning	55–
cannot be touched by death, and even so he sins.	56
If you are comforted at[60] his [Adam's] formation, you will learn,	131–
that he was formed mortal, as well as immortal.	132
With his freedom a rational harbour was granted to him,	141–
to choose [between] death and life by his free will.	142
Thus, the cause of his death was in him, since he is from dust,	157–
and likewise he had the option for life, for his soul is a spirit.	158
If he had become victorious and chosen to become immortal,	159–
the soul would have pulled the body to live with it.	160
The weak one lost and with his weakness he inclined to death.	161
And after [his] free choice picked the fruit from the tree,	197–
death defeated him, who would not die if he had kept [the commandment].	198
He [the Creator] put the reason/cause of life and the love of death in his hand,	279–
and granted him the option to draw near towards what he wishes.	280
If He had made him immortal at the beginning,	281–
he would be lost after having trespassed against the commandment.	282

---

[60] E ܥܩܒܬܐ, inquire into.

And if somehow He had created him mortal, such as animals, what would he benefit from keeping the commandment?	283– 284
Therefore, it is beautiful/great that he became mortal and immortal, and granted the power of free will upon both of them."	285– 286

After the long opening speech (line 1–20), Jacob identifies the theme of the *memro* with the words: *Grant me to speak on whether You created Adam mortal or truly immortal as the highests* (line 21–22). He clarifies his topic pointing out that his approach is not prying into the divine nature of the Creator, but asking about the nature of the created Adam in his primordial state (23–38). The rest of the *memro* is basically the answer to the two causal questions (39–42) and the explanation of the following two causal sentences (43–46) expressed by Jacob that are found at the beginning of the citation identified by John of Dara. The questions refer to the relation of the divine commandments to the mortality and/or immortality of man.

The citation by John also includes the next two couplets (47–50) and lines 55–56, which provide an indirect answer to the questions. In line 47, Jacob begins with the acclamation "behold" (ܗܐ) and refers in the following to creation, emphasising that the nature of created beings does not change. The angels, such as Gabriel, do not become mortal, even if they had trespassed against the commandments of the Lord. Satan, too, does not become mortal, even though he trespasses frequently against the Creator. In turn all sorts of animals die even though they do not have any commandment to disobey. In 57–76 Jacob explores this argument further, but John of Dara leaves it out.

From line 77 onwards Jacob focuses on human nature, which differs from all other created beings, which are either mortal or immortal. John leaves out Jacob's long introduction and dialogue with the audience, as he places the listeners in position of judges to decide about truth, in the same way as Jacob emphasises the role of man's free will that has the power, as its Creator, to decide about its mortality and immortality. John focuses selectively on the important passages, and leaves out Jacob's long explanations, metaphors and allusions to nature. From the couplets 131/2, 141/2, 157/8, 159/60 and line 161, which John quotes, it becomes clear that man was created mortal, as well as immortal: mortal because of his bodily formation out of the earth, and immortal due to his spiritual soul. Either of them had the power to pull the other to its side. Man's free will was there to make the decision.

Next John quotes the couplet where Jacob explicitly expresses the decision taken by man's free will with the fact that man's mortality became victorious over his immortality (197/8). And finally, John quotes from the end four couplets where Jacob summarises his point (279–286) that Adam was created mortal (ܡܝܘܬܐ), as well as immortal (ܠܐ ܡܝܘܬܐ). Mortality (ܡܝܘܬܘܬܐ) and everlasting life (ܚܝܐ) were part of the human being and were attributed to the free will of man (ܨܒܝܢܐ).[61]

Thus, Jacob compares the nature of created beings, such as the angles and animals, with the nature of human body to show that Adam was created both mortal as well as immortal. Both mortality as well as immortality were given as a choice to human free will. The reason given to the commandment is found in this previous intermediate state of Adam, which is described as a battle in which Adam would become victorious or would be defeated according to his free will.

In the following, John cites from other authors and focuses on the immortality of the body by grace (ܒܛܝܒܘܬܐ), by deeds (ܒܣܘܥܪܢܐ), and by divine power (ܒܚܝܠܐ ܐܠܗܝܐ). At the end of chapter three, John quotes from Cyril of Alexandrian mentioning Plato and his philosophical theory on the immortality of sun, moon and stars that are supposed to possess a soul. Following Cyril, John rejects such teaching.[62]

The text quoted by John illustrates mainly minor differences to Jacob text. John quoted carefully and selected systematically the stances he needed for his account. The differences found in the texts are not necessarily caused by John. They could be partly due to the text he used, or due to the copyists after him. Following table lists the variations:

---

[61] MS Mardin 137 (= **E**), Memro 81, fol. 242v.
[62] A 48r, B 64r–64v, C 179–80.

	Line	John of Dara	Jacob of Serugh
Pa'el—'apa'el	282	ܐܟܬܒ	ܟܬܒ
Participle active—imperfect	56	ܢܫܒܚ	ܡܫܒܚ
Participle passive—imperfect	56	ܢܬܩܪܒ	ܡܬܩܪܒ
Sequence of words	55	ܠܐ ܣܒܪܐ ܡܢ ܥܒܪ	ܡܢ ܥܒܪ ܠܐ ܣܒܪܐ (E) ܠܐ ܣܒܪܐ ܡܢ ܥܒܪ (Alwan)
	279	ܠܓܠܝܐ ܚܙܝܐ ܘܠܟܣܝܐ ܡܬܓܫܫ	ܠܚܙܝܐ ܓܠܝܐ ܘܠܡܬܓܫܫ ܟܣܝܐ (E) ܠܚܙܝܐ ܓܠܝܐ ܘܠܟܣܝܐ ܡܬܓܫܫ (Alwan)
Adverb	41	ܡܛܟܣܐܝܬ	ܡܛܟܣܐܝܬ
Vocabularies	50	ܢܟܬܘܒ	ܢܪܫܘܡ (Alwan)
	131	ܬܬܠܡܕ	ܬܠܡܝܕܐ
	161	ܫܪܝܪ	ܬܩܢ
	161	ܬܩܢ	ܫܪܝܪ
	197	ܒܪܝܐ	ܒܪܝܐ (Alwan)
Prepositions	141	ܡܢ	ܥܠ
	160	ܠܗ	ܒܗ
Suffix ending	40	ܥܒܕܐ	ܥܒܕܗ (Alwan)
	45	ܥܒܕܗ	ܥܒܕܐ (Alwan)
	141	ܫܘܒܚܗ	ܬܫܒܘܚܬܐ
Prefix	157	ܬܚܬ ܪܓܠܘܗܝ	ܬܚܬ ܠܪܓܠܘܗܝ
	160	ܕܟܝܢܐ	ܠܟܝܢܐ
Position of ܕ	47	ܗܘܐ ܡܢܗܘܢ ܠܐ ܣܒܪܐ ܘܠܐ ܥܒܪ ܡܢ ܐܬܦܩܪ	ܗܘܐ ܣܦܩ ܕܠܐ ܡܢܗܘܢ ܡܢ ܐܬܦܩܪ

	Line	John of Dara	Jacob of Serugh
ܘ—copula	50	ܘܠܐ	ܠܐ
Gender	44	ܬܚܝܬܗ	ܬܚܝܬܗ

While some of the varieties are due to orthographical variations, or differences in sequence of words, other differences occur in prepositions, vocabulary, prefixes or suffixes. It is also noticeable that four verbs appear in different forms and some nouns in different status. Despite these variations, John of Dara cites literarily from Jacob of Serugh. His citations are chosen very carefully. Therefore, John must have had a copy of this verse-homily of Jacob.

3.2. Homily on Adam's expulsion from Paradise

Vööbus identified Jacob's verse-homily *On Adam`s Expulsion from Paradise* in the manuscripts London British Library Add. 17215 and Add 12169, Sharfeh Patr. 312, Mardin Syrian-orth. Patr. 137 and Dair Za'faran (A).[63] Except the first fragments, Alwan made use of all these manuscripts in his edition.[64] In comparison to Alwan's edition, I followed MS Mardin 137 [**E**][65]. John of Dara refers to this verse-homily in his treatises.[66]

Jacob's verse-homily *On Adam's expulsion from Paradise* deals with the cause of Adam's departure from Paradise. This question

---

[63] Vööbus, A. *Handschriftliche Überlieferung der Memre-Dichtung des Ja`qob von Serug*, III, 72, 155–57, CSCO, 421; Subsidia, 60, Louvain, 1980; II, 23; IV, 33.

[64] Alwan, *Jacques de Saroug*, xviii, 31–77; translation 33–86.

[65] This verse-homily is *memro* 282 in MS Mardin 137 (= **E**), folio 243r–256v. The incipit is: ܐܠܗܐ ܐܒܐ ܒܪܝܟ ܗܘ ܡܢ ܒܪܝܫܝܬ. Similar incipit can be found by Assemanus, J.S. *Bibliotheca Orientalis Clementino-Vaticana*, I, Rome, 1719, homily number 228 (ܐܠܗܐ ܐܒܐ ܒܪܝܟ ܠܐܒܘܢ ܡܢ ܒܪܝܫܝܬ), p. 305–40; see Brock, S.P. "The published verse Homilies of Isaac of Antioch, Jacob of Serugh, and Narsai: Index of Incipits," *JSS* 32,2 (Autumn 1987): 296.

[66] John of Dara refers to this *memro* in A 13r, 21v, 34r; B 12r, 24v–25r, 43r; C 38, 72, 121 [E 245r, 255v–256r, 253v–254r].

leads also to the cause of evil. Jacob dismisses the theory of relating fault to the Creator, or to the nature of the creation. He attributes the cause of expulsion to man's free will. Neither the nature of spiritual beings, like those of the angel, nor the created nature of human beings is the reason for sin and evil. From the angel he refers to Satan, whose nature is the same as all the other angels; however, he sinned due to his free will. Concerning human beings, Jacob refers to Judas Iscariot who was one of the twelve disciples, but betrayed Jesus aching out of his free will. Therefore, neither the Creator nor the creation can be blamed.[67]

In this context Jacob focuses on Adam's nature. Jacob dismisses the idea that Adam was a child and not mature enough to know what he was doing. Adam was not a child[68], because he desired to become God and he was actively involved in achieving it. Giving names to the animals is one proof of Adam's knowledge and maturity.[69] Thus, it was Adam's fault, but he was influenced by Satan. Satan fell and caused Adam to fall with him. As Adam fell deeply, he was not able to get up by himself, except through divine mercy. God's love created Adam, not to be expelled out of Paradise, but to inherit the heavenly kingdom by his victory.[70] Jacob emphasises the intermediate state of mortality and immortality, the possibility of sinning and not sinning. As the nature of Satan and Adam were not evil, neither the nature of the Serpent, nor of the trees in Paradise, including their fruits, were bad. Creation is not the reason and source of Adam's spiritual and natural death. In his battle against humanity, however, Satan used the Serpent, as well as the Tree of Knowledge, as a tool to mislead mankind.[71]

---

[67] E 243v–244v.

[68] E 244v (stances 107–8): ܐܢ ܫܒܪܐ ܗܘܐ ܐܕܡ ܐܦ ܠܐ ܐܕܝܩ ܐܠܗܐ. ܐܠܐ ܝܕܥ ܗܘܐ ܕܡܪܝܡ ܥܠ ܦܘܩܕܢܐ.

[69] E 244v (stances 117–8): ܐܢ ܫܒܪܐ ܠܐ ܝܕܥ ܗܘܐ ܫܒܪܐ. ܐܬܐ ܥܡ ܗܘܐ ܫܡܗܐ ܠܟܠ ܚܝܘܬܐ ܕܐܝܬ ܒܗ̇.

[70] E 245r (stances 169–70): ܒܚܘܒܗ̇ ܗܘܐ ܒܪܝ ܠܐ ܗܘܐ ܕܢܦܘܩ ܡܢ ܦܪܕܝܣܐ. ܐܠܐ ܕܢܐܪܬ ܗܘܐ ܗܝܢ ܐܘ ܡܠܟܘ.

[71] E 246r–247v.

Eve could have won the battle against Satan, but because she liked what she heard and desired to become divine, priest and superior to her husband, she did not question the Serpent and ate the fruit. For Jacob, Mary questioning the angel is evidence that women's nature is not deprived of wisdom and victory. Eve could easily have become victorious over Satan, because he did not have anymore to say.[72]

Then Jacob focuses on the clothing of man's nakedness with fig leaves and with the garment they later put on. Losing their garment of glory, Adam and Eve felt ashamed and hid themselves. Jacob interprets the sound of God's footsteps, His question to Adam and His question to Eve, as three opportunities for Adam to become penitent.[73]

Presenting man's free will as the cause of evil, Jacob explains at great length why the Serpent and the earth were cursed, since they did have not free will, and naturally they are good created beings.[74]

John of Dara refers twice explicitly to this *memro* of Jacob of Serugh and quotes from it. In chapter seven of *memro* two that is *On Creation*, John cites 32 to 34 lines from this verse-homily, while he talks about the nature of the Serpent. John refuses the theory that God granted the gift of language and knowledge (ܡܠܠܬܐ ܘܝܕܥܬܐ) to the Serpent. John points out that Satan talked through the Serpent, using the following citation from Jacob:[75]

ܒܡܘܬܒ ܕܝܢ ܕܦܠܓ ܒܡܐܡܪܐ ܕܥܠ ܡܦܩܬܗ ܕܐܕܡ ܡܢ ܦܪܕܝܣܐ
ܐܡܪ. ܕܣܛܢܐ ܡܠܠ ܒܚܘܝܐ. ܗܘ ܕܠܗ ܫܠܡܝܢ ܘܣܠܩ. ܐܡܪ ܓܝܪ.

839– ܒܝܬ ܒܒܪܝܬܐ ܗܕܐ ܡܦܪܫܝܢ ܒܗ̇[76] ܦܩ̈ܚܝܢ܇
840 ܕܗܘܐ ܠܗ ܚܘܝܐ ܐܝܟ ܠܫܢܐ[77] ܒܕܪܫܬܗ.

[72] E 247v–49v
[73] E 250v–253r.
[74] E 253r–254r.
[75] A 21v; B 24v–25r; C 72; [E 253v–254r, page 22–23 of the *memro*].
[76] ܒܗ̇: Alwan ܒܗ.
[77] ܠܫܢܐ: A ܠܫܢܗ.

Jacob of Serugh and His Influence

	.	841–
	.	842
	[80]	843–
	.	844
[These two lines are missing by John of Dara.]	.	845–
	.	846
	.	847–
	[86]	848
	.	849–
	.	850
	.	851–
	.	852
	.	853–
	.	854
	.	855–
	.	856
	.	857–
[These two lines are missing by JD]	.	858

---

[78] : Alwan, E .
[79] : ABC is missing.
[80] : Alwan, E .
[81] : Alwan, E .
[82] : Alwan, E .
[83] : Alwan .
[84] : Alwan, E .
[85] : Alwan .
[86] : Alwan, E .
[87] B add : AE missing.

859–	.... ⁸⁸
860	⁸⁹
861–	⁹⁰ ⁹¹
862	⁹² ⁹³
863–	
864	⁹⁴
865–	⁹⁵
866	⁹⁶

[These four lines are missing by JD.]

867–	
868	
869–	
870	
871–	⁹⁷ ⁹⁸
872	⁹⁹
873–	⁾¹⁰⁰
874	¹⁰¹

---

⁸⁸ : B .

⁸⁹ : Alwan, E (John makes one line out of the couplet found by Jacob).

⁹⁰ : E .

⁹¹ : B .

⁹² : A is very difficult to read, but it could be . Alwan has got too.

⁹³ : E .

⁹⁴ : B .

⁹⁵ : B .

⁹⁶ : E ; Alwan .

⁹⁷ : Alwan, E .

⁹⁸ : Alwan, E .

⁹⁹ : Alwan, E .

¹⁰⁰ : Alwan, E .

¹⁰¹ : Alwan, E .

	875–	ܕܠܐ ܢܒܙ ܗܘܘ ܚܠܝܢ ܠܡܐܟܘܠܬܐ.[102]
	876	ܐܠܐ ܠܡܐܟܘܠܬܐ ܕܬܨܒܘܬܗ ܠܚܝܐ ܢܩܝܡܘܗ݀.
	877–	ܗܘܗܕܐ ܕܐܬܕܠܝܘ[103] ܒܦܐܪܐ.
	878	ܒܗ ܡܠܝܐ[104] ܕܬܗܘܐ ܗܘܐ ܠܗܘܢ[105].
[These	879–	ܫܪܝ ܟܪܙܘܬܐ ܘܬܐܘܕܝܬܐ ܠܥܡܐ ܗܘܐ.
six lines	880	ܕܡܬܒܠܗܘܢ ܗܘܐ ܠܚܕܐ ܕܐܝܟ ܗܘ ܐܢܝܘܝ.
are	881–	ܠܘܐܙܠ ܕܐܬܦܩܪ ܒܓܗܘܡܐ ܢܟܪܝܐ ܘܠܗ ܩܕܝ,ܗܡ..
missing	882	ܘܐܬܕܟܪܬܝܗܝ ܗܘܐ ܒܠܘܚܬܗ ܥܡ ܕܓܠܗ.
by JD.]	883–	ܒܠܕ ܗܘܐ ܙܘܒܐ ܪܒܐ ܕܢܘܪܢܐ ܕܘܡܗܕ ܠܫܩܠ|.
	884	ܡܠܐ ܠܣܘܒܐ ܕܙܘܡܐ ܪܘܡܐ ܒܚܕܐ.
	885–	ܕܚܘܒܐ[106] ܐܬܕܠܝ ܗܘ ܕܙܘܒܐ ܚܠܠ ܕܐܬܚܕܗ..
	886	ܒܗ[107] ܐܪܟܠ ܗܘܐ ܘܒܗ ܡܓܠ ܗܘܐ ܠܗ ܙܪ ܐܒܠܟ֎

Jacob of Badnan, however, said in his verse-homily *On Adam's Expulsion from Paradise*, that Satan talked through the Serpent. We agree with this. He said so:

The Hebrews interpret this with objections,	839
namely that the Serpent mislead Eve with his cunning;	840
so that Satan did not betray her with his free will,	841–
and therefore he [Serpent] was cursed by justice.	842
If there were a fellow-friend with him, while he mislead,	843–
the Righteous One would curse him with justice, as He did	844
to the Serpent.	

---

[102] ܕܠܐ ܢܒܙ ܗܘܘ ܚܠܝܢ ܠܡܐܟܘܠܬܐ: Alwan, E ܕܗ ܠܐ ܢܒܙ ܗܘܘ ܠܗܘܢ ܚܠܝܢ ܠܡܐܟܘܠܬܐ.

[103] ܕܐܬܕܠܝܘ ܒܦܐܪܐ ܗܘܐ: Alwan, E ܕܐܝܟܢ ܗܘܗܕܐ ܕܐܬܕܠܝܘ ܒܦܐܪܐ ܗܘܐ ܐܠܐ.

[104] ܒܗ: Alwan, E ܕܒ.

[105] ܒܗ ܡܠܝܐ ܕܬܗܘܐ ܗܘܐ ܠܗܘܢ: Alwan, E ܕܒ ܡܠܝܐ ܕܬܗܘܐ ܗܘܐ ܠܗܘܢ ܕܐܘܪܚܐ.

[106] ܕܚܘܒܐ: Alwan, E ܕܚܘܒܐ.

[107] ܒܗܘ: Alwan, E ܒܗ.

And he [Jacob] said against them:

So now let lie close the mouth of the one who spoke false, and let truth come near to tell its opinion without shame.	*[Missing by John of Dara]*	845–846
He, who would think that that was Eve's error only, is a common fellow of the evil one and his protector.		847–848
From the fact that the Serpent was cursed, one should learn, that the deception that he planted there belonged to someone else.	*[Missing by John of Dara]*	849–850
As the earth was cursed by mercy because of Adam, in the same way the Serpent was cursed in wrath because of the evil one.		851–852
Earth neither possessed ignorance nor freedom; likewise the Serpent did not have free will, nor deception.		853–854
If it is because the Serpent has been cursed there, [one would think] he [the Serpent] mislead, then it must had been the earth that ate from the tree.		855–856
He [God] cursed the earth because Adam acted foolishly, and He cursed the Serpent because of the evil one who deceived.		857–858
And the curse of the earth is that of Adam, and the curse of the Serpent is that of the evil one.[108]		859–860
When the Lord cursed the earth, He made Adam suffer. And when He threatened the Serpent, He provoked anger in the evil one.		861–862

---

[108] John of Dara makes out of one couplet one line. Alwan, E: While all curse of the earth belongs to Adam, so too the curse of the Serpent belongs to the evil one.

He crushed the flute that brings pain upon its player,		863–
and the *guitar* that throws lamentation upon its holder.		864

He tied the horse that stupefied its horseman,		865–
and he turned over the ship that caused harm to its sailor.		866

He cursed the furnace in which the deceitful word was fabricated,	*[Missing by John of Dara]*	867–868
to increase the pain of the craftsman who blew into it.		

He broke the bow that bent and gave birth to Adam's death,	869–870
to become feeble and fall from its holder, and to make him feel sorry too.	

He is the one who caused life to [have pity on] the horse,	871–
in order to keep his rider alive to insult him.	872

The mount [horse] getting wounded by the bowman, while	873–
he did not made mistake, so that he who is riding on will fall in the battle.	874

Although the horse is not liable to a blued feud against the	875–
warrior, he shoots against him, so that through his fall he will thrust down his owner.	876

Likewise, when the Serpent was cursed, Satan was insulted	877–
through him [Serpent].[109]	878

The [divine] justice shot warlike against the Serpent,	*[Missing by John of Dara]*	879–880
for she was swift to the adversary as he became victorious through her.		

The curses came out in the likeness of the arrows and pierced him [Serpent], and its swiftness fell lame because of his deceit.	881–882

The mount [horse] was bitten so that perturbation falls upon his rider. He [God] cursed the Serpent to put in Satan alarums.	883–884

---

[109] Also here John summarises the couplet in one line. Alwan, E: Like this the Serpent was cursed by God, as Satan was insulted by justice.

Cursing the Serpent [means] cursing the one who talked through the Serpent there,	885– 886
and he [Satan] led astray through him [Serpent], and received sentence [of punishment] through him.	

For Jacob, cursing the Serpent does not prove that Adam's expulsion was the Serpent's fault. With various references to natural metaphors and biblical allusions he clarifies this. Following the quotation John presents Jacob's teaching representative for all church fathers, as he summarises: "In the same way all the blessed teachers of the church say, that Satan spoke through the Serpent".[110] Thus, John summarises Jacob's teaching as representative for all church fathers.

Without quoting anymore from Jacob in this passage, John continues and emphasises jealousy (ܚܣܡܐ) as the main reason for Satan causing man to fall, for man was created out of dust in the image and likeness of God. While Satan fell and was expelled, Adam joined the angelic world in Paradise. This is the reasons given for Satan's jealousy.

Without explicitly mentioning this verse-homily, at the end of chapter eight of *memro* three that is *On the Tree of Life*, John makes further use of Jacob's ideas. John paraphrases Jacob's reasoning and alters it. Jacob's concern is on the role of women, i.e. Eve who could have acted like Mary and questioned what she was told. The argument should have been between Eve and the Serpent. John transfers the same account and locates it between Adam and Eve, so that Adam should have been wise and questions Eve's words and deeds. For instance, according to Jacob, Eve could have said to the Serpent:[111]

471–	ܐܢ ܗܘ ܗܝ, ܐܝܟ ܕܐܡܪܬ ܐܢܬ ܡܠܠ ܚܝܐ
472	ܠܐ ܣܢܝܩ ܠܝ ܐܠܘܗܝܬܐ ܕܝܗܒ ܐܢܬ ܠܝ
473–	ܠܡܐ ܠܐ ܐܦܠܘ ܐܢܬ ܩܝܡ ܡܢ ܐܠܗܐ.
474	ܘܗܘܢܟ ܥܠܝܟ ܗܘ ܐܬܐ ܕܠܐ ܢܡܘܣ.

---

[110] A 21v; B25r; C 72:

ܗܟܢ ܟܠܗܘܢ ܡܠܦܢܐ ܛܘܒܬܢܐ ܕܥܕܬܐ. ܐܡܪܝܢ ܣܛܢܐ ܐܡܪ ܒܗ ܒܚܘܝܐ.

[111] E 249r; Alwan, 52.

471– 472	If it is so as you say, why has divinity, which you are aware of, not been granted to you?
473– 474	Why have not you eaten from the tree first, and became God, and then reveal it to me to eat too?

John writes that Adam could have said to Eve:[112]

ܕܗ̇ܐ ܐܢܬܝ، ܐܟܠܬܝ، ܘܠܐ ܗܘܝܬܝ، [113] ܐܠܗܬܐ. ܘܠܐ ܙܕܩ ܕܐܥܒܪ
ܥܠ ܦܘܩܕܢܗ ܕܐܠܗܐ. ܡܝܬܪܐܝܬ ܕܠܐ ܫܘܐ ܐܢܐ ܚܙܐ ܡ̣ܢ ܠܟ̈ܝ
ܠܘܬܟܝ ܕܐܟܠܬܝ، [114] ܘܠܐ ܠܘܬ ܚܘܝܐ ܕܐܡ̣ܪ ܠܟܝ ܕܗܘܝܬܝ، [115]
ܐܠܗܬܐ. ܗ̣ܘ ܙܕܩ ܗ̣ܘܐ ܕܢܐܟܘܠ ܩܕܡܐܝܬ ܘܢܗܘܐ ܐܠܗܐ. ܘܟܢ
ܐܢܬܝ ܕܐܟܠܬܝ، [116] ܙܕܩ ܗ̣ܘܐ ܕܬܬܐܠܗܬ، [117] . ܐܠܐ ܠܐ ܗ̣ܘܝܬܝ،
ܐܠܗܐ.

Behold, you have eaten and did not become God. I should not transgress God's commandment, for especially I do not see any benefits for you who have already eaten, neither for the Serpent who told you that you will become God. [The Serpent] was supposed to eat first and become God, and then you who ate were supposed to become divine. However, you did not become God.

Here one can see how John makes use of material found in Jacob's verse-homilies. In this context John talks about non-physical nature, irrational natures and the nature of human beings that all three of them utter praises to God in different ways. John develops Jacob's theology, and speaks of different stages that human nature can achieve: it can be rational in the likeness of God and praise God by the motion of mind and knowledge, it can be in the likeness of animals and become irrational, but it can also become like the devils, falling into error and evil. According to John, at the beginning Adam was praising God with the words of a

---

112 A 53r; B 72r; C 200.

113 ܕܗ̇ܐ ܐܢܬܝ، ܐܟܠܬܝ، ܘܠܐ ܗܘܝܬܝ، : C ܕܗ̇ܐ ܐܢܬܝ ܐܟܠܬܝ ܘܠܐ ܗܘܝܬܝ.

114 ܠܘܬܟܝ ܕܐܟܠܬܝ، : C ܠܘܬܟܝ ܕܐܟܠܬܝ.

115 ܕܗܘܝܬܝ، : C ܕܗܘܝܬܝ.

116 ܕܐܟܠܬܝ، : C ܕܐܟܠܬܝ.

117 ܕܬܬܐܠܗܬ، : C ܕܐܬܐܠܗܬ، .

pure mind (ܗܘܢܐ ܕܟܝܐ), not with the words of the human tongue. However, while Satan was driven by jealousy to bring man to fall, man was driven by desire to become God. John concludes his chapter on the Tree of Life pointing out that man's loss of Paradise is because Adam and Eve desired to become divine and "desired Divinity" (ܪܓ ܐܠܗܘܬܐ).[118]

After Jacob comments on Adam's action and their punishment at great length, he reaches the end of Genesis 3, that is the biblical passage where God sent Adam and Eve forth from Paradise (Gen 3:20–24). Jacob found the title of his *memro* from this biblical passage, and ends with it. Referring to the skin garments that God made for man (Gen 3:21), Jacob points out that God's action stems from compassion, mercy and love. This is in contrast to before, where God imposed punishment by justice (Gen 3:14–19). At the end of the *memro*, Jacob focuses explicitly on God's intention and emphasises His merciful act.

John agrees with such an interpretation and cites eleven lines in the second *memro*, chapter eleven that is entitled *On the Garments of Skin that God made for Adam* (Gen 3:21).[119]

---

[118] A 53r; B 72r; C 201.

[119] A 34r; B 43r–43v; C 121–122; [E 255v–257r, page 26–27 of the *memro*].

Jacob of Serugh and his influence

[These two lines   999–   .
are missing by   1000   .
JD.]   .

1006   .   [Missing by JD.]
1007–   [Missing partly
1009   .   by JD.]

---

[120] : E .
[121] : Alwan .
[122] : Alwan, BE .
[123] : Alwan .
[124] : Alwan .
[125] : Alwan, E .
[126] : AC .
[127] : Alwan, E .
[128] : Alwan .
[129] : B . B read the first character as an because the in A is illegible.
[130] : Alwan (mistake).

	¹³¹ ܡܢ ܠܐ ܐܝܟܢ ܠܐܠ ܕܟܣܝܬܐ ܠܘܬܗ ܐܘܦ ܐܠܗܐ.	[1007–1009]
[These five lines are missing by JD.]	ܠܐ ܐܚܕ ܢܦܫܗ ܗܘܘ ܕܠܚܡܬ ܗܘܘ ܒܗ ܐܦܠܐ.	1010
	ܒܪܐ ܕܒܪܝܗ ܗܘ ܕܩܕܡܝܐ ܘܕܒܬܪܟܢ ܗܘܐ.	1011–
	ܠܐ ܐܚܒܨܗ ܕܠܐ ܟܕ ܥܪܛܠ ܗܘܐ ܠܒܪ ܢܫܕܝܘܗܝ.	1012
	ܓܠܓ ܗܘܘ ܠܗ ܙܩܘܪܐ ܕܟܐܡܬ ܕܒܐܝܕܝ ܐܠܗܐ. ¹³²	1013–
	ܘܐܣܠܛܝܘܗܝ ܠܦܓܪܢܐ ܕܠܐ ܢܗܘܘܢ ܒܗ ܕܠܗܝܢ.	1014
	ܩܛܝܢ ܠܗܘܢ ¹³³ ܐܝܟ ܣܪܝܩܐ ܡܢ ܠܐ ܡܕܡ.	1015–
	ܘܩܛܝܒ ܠܗܘܢ ܐܝܟ ܕܠܐܢܫ ܡܠܐܠ ܐܣܟܡܗܘܢ.	1016

Jacob of Badnan says, when the Creator felt sorry for them:	
He did not grasp firmly to throw them out [of Paradise] naked.	996
He weaved garments out of nothing, and clothed them, so that their nakedness became sheltered.	997– 998
[Although] it is written so: He made garments of skin (Gen 3:21), [still] this is all a request by the listeners. *[Missing by John of Dara]*	999– 1000
The Creator gave a sign for making clothes out of nothing, and because it [clothes] felt thick, he called it skin.	1001– 1002
He prepared it on their bodies, and He did not weave it on another web and then they put it on.	1003– 1004
The [divine] sign fabricated it swiftly upon their bodies.	1005–
He weaved and stretched it out beautifully upon their bodies. *[Missing by John of Dara]*	1006

---

¹³¹ ܐܝܟܢ : AC ܐܝܢܐ; Alwan ܐܝܢܘ. John composed this line out the last three lines of Jacob of Serugh (1007–1009).

¹³² ܒܐܝܕܝ : Alwan ܒܐܝܕܝ.

¹³³ ܠܗܘܢ ܛܒ: E ܠܗܘܢ ܗܘܐ ܛܒ.

They did not feel it while it was put on them by Creator,	*[Partly missing by John of Dara.]*	1007–1009
since He did not bring it from another place and put it on them.		
Until they touched the garments and saw them		
Without feeling/touching they put on the garments and saw them.		[1007–1009]
they did not know that they had clothes on under the trees.	*[Missing by John of Dara.]*	1010–1014
Until they saw the bareness that was covered [before],		
they did not realise that there were no leaves on their bodies.		
The mercy of [God's] act of creation touched the naked people,		
and their nakedness put on garments out of nothing.		
He was driving them out of His house like thieves,		1015–1016
and putting [clothes] on them like children because of His grace.		

Even God expelled Adam and Eve from Paradise as "thieves" (ܓܢܒܐ), as Jacob says, but He made garments of skin for them out of nothing to cover them mercifully as "children" (ܒܢܝܐ). One can see in the single line after the citation from Jacob, how much John values Jacob's thoughts. John summarises what Jacob explored in his verse-homily in a single sentence and approves it: "With His love He put on them [clothes], and then drove them out [of Paradise]" (ܒܚܘܒܗ ܐܠܒܫ ܐܢܘܢ ܘܗܝܕܝܢ ܐܦܩ ܐܢܘܢ).[134] After that

---

[134] ܒܚܘܒܗ ܐܠܒܫ ܐܢܘܢ ܘܗܝܕܝܢ ܐܦܩ ܐܢܘܢ: This sentence is not a literal citation, but a summary of what follows by Jacob of Serugh [1018–1026]:

ܗܘܘ ܡܬܒܝܢܝܢ ܒܬܘܠܬܐ ܡܢ ܐܝܟܐ ܐܬܟܣܝܘ܂
ܘܐܡܪܗ ܐܢܫܘܬܐ ܠܚܘܒܐ ܪܒܐ ܥܠ ܛܠܝܘܬܐ܂
ܠܐܕܡ ܐܒܘܟ ܬܘܒ ܚܙܝܗܝ ܐܢܘܢ ܕܗܐ ܟܠܗܘܢ܂
ܘܡܚܒܢ ܩܝܡܝܢ ܐܢܘܢ ܕܠܒܫ ܐܢܘܢ ܒܚܘܒܬܐ܂
ܡܗܦܟ ܠܗܘܢ ܡܢ ܦܪܕܝܣܐ ܐܝܟ ܕܠܓܢܒܐ܂

John finishes this chapter with a reference to Athanasius' *memro On Crucifixion.*

Mentioning Jacob's name once more, John refers again explicitly to this verse-homily, whereby he paraphrases what Jacob says and does not cite it literally. The reference is very brief and appears at the end of the first *memro*, chapter five that *demonstrates an Opinion on Paradise.*[135] The passage in Jacob's *memro* points out that the Creator and creation can not be blamed for Adam's disobedience and his expulsion from Paradise. Adam was created to stay in Paradise and not to be thrown out. John, however, paraphrases Jacob's text in the context, when he talks about marriage and mankind being fruitful and multiplying the earth (Gen 1:29). John writes:[136]

ܘܐܦ ܝܥܩܘܒ ܕܒܛܢܢ ܒܡܐܡܪܐ ܕܡܦܩܬܗ ܕܐܕܡ ܡܢ ܦܪܕܝܣܐ ܐܡܪ.
ܒܪܝܗ܆ ܗܟܝܠ ܡܪܝܐ ܠܐܕܡ ܠܗ̇ ܕܢܦܩܘܢ ܡܢ ܦܪܕܝܣܐ
ܐܠܐ ܕܢܫܬܠܛ ܒܗ ܘܢܗܘܐ ܝܪܬܐ ܕܝܠܗ.[137]

"And also Jacob of Batnan said in the *memro On Adams expulsion from Paradise*:
Thus, the Lord created Adam, not to drive him out of Paradise,
but to have dominion over it and become its heir.

4. CONCLUSION

John of Dara's rich references to previous authors witness the intellectual movements of the ninth century AD, a time when scientific knowledge of the ancient world was collected and

ܘܡܠܟ ܐܝܕܗ ܥܠ ܦܘܪܫܢܘܗܝ ܫܒܝܚܐܝܬ.
ܫܘܒܚܐ ܦܬܝܟ ܗܘܐ ܒܟܢܪ ܕܒܠܗ ܙܥܘܪܐܝܬ܆
ܕܐܠܒܫ ܐܢܘܢ ܘܥܛܦܝܢ ܐܝܟ ܠܦܘܪܕ ܐܢܘܢ.
ܒܪܚܡܘܬܗ ܡܟܠܝܐ ܗܘܬ ܡܢ ܡܪܕܘܬܗ܆
ܕܠܟܢܫܐ ܠܒܘܫܐ ܪܒ ܗܘܐ ܡܢ ܕܐܬܒܢܝܬܗ.

[135] [ܒܡܐܠܬܐ AB] ܘܡܠܘܐܢ ܕܫܡܥܐ܆ ܡܚܘܐ ܡܚܘܝܢܘܬܐ ܕܥܠ ܦܪܕܝܣܐ; A 11r; B 8r; C 30.

[136] A 13r; B 12r; C 38; [E 245].

[137] ܕܝܠܗ ܝܪܬܐ: A ܝܪܬܗ. E 245 [line 169–170]
ܒܪܝܗ܆ ܗܘܐ ܡܪܝܐ ܠܐ ܗܘܐ ܕܢܦܩܘܢ ܡܢ ܦܪܕܝܣܐ܆
ܐܠܐ ܕܢܚܘܠ ܢܗܘܐ ܝܪܬܐ ܐܦ ܥܠܝܬܐ.

presented in a systematic order as a compendium. John of Dara's theological themes, such as Paradise, Creator and creation, mortality and immortality, must have been of great relevance and a response to the intellectual questions of his time.

In the Islamic Golden Age, John of Dara chooses his topics carefully, deals with the themes thoroughly, and presents his material systematically. Being concerned about the theology of creation and resurrection in the context of salvation—probably in its distinctive significance from non-Christian and agnostic teachings—John's treatises present an anthropological Christian approach in accordance with the teaching of the church fathers. He tries to find a synthesis between the different teachings of the church fathers. Among them, Jacob of Serugh stands up as one of the most prominent authorities whom John of Dara often follows.

John must have had access to Jacob's verse-homilies. The citations quoted above demonstrate how John refers to Jacob of Serugh and how he presents Jacob's theological teaching on subjects dealt with. Referring to Jacob, John often mentions the name and the sources he used. With this information it becomes easy to identify the cited passages. John's citations of Jacob's verse-homilies proved very accurate, even though the references differ in style. Some of the citations are long as they present an important part of a verse-homily; other long passages are put together from a number of couplets that together present a central message. In such a case, John focuses on the main topic, leaving out the long explorations, allusions, metaphors and repetitions found by Jacob. At other times, John summarises Jacob's teaching, either by focusing on a few couplets, or by putting the meaning in his own words as a synthesis. Furthermore, occasionally John makes use of Jacobs's material without mentioning Jacob's name, as he transfers and adopts the ideas, found by Jacob, into his own context.

Further work on John of Dara's work could identify more ideas and themes, which have been taken from Jacob without explicit reference to him. In comparison, identifying the texts and citations of the other authors, to whom John of Dara refers to, would provide better knowledge on both: on John of Dara, how he incorporates the work of previous writers in his treatises; and on Jacob of Serugh's authority in comparison to the other authors.

www.ingramcontent.com/pod-product-compliance
Lightning Source LLC
Chambersburg PA
CBHW071231160426
43196CB00012B/2485